LEFT: The ancient sanctuary knocker. By grasping it, fugitives from the law could find safety in Holy Trinity Church for 37 days before facing trial. ①

The Reformation saw many changes to what had been created in the preceding years. In 1547, the College was closed on the instructions of King Henry VIII, its assets being given to the town. No trace of its building now remains. The rood and chantry chapels were abolished, much of the glass was destroyed and the carving damaged.

In 1675 a wooden spire was added to the tower, to be replaced in 1763 by the elegant stone spire we see today.

During the 19th century many additions to the church were put in place. Notable products of an early Victorian emphasis on the preaching of the Word were the side galleries in the nave aisles, box pews and three-decker pulpit. By 1885 these had gone. The choir stalls were brought forward from the tower and later both chancel and nave were re-floored, the whole effect being to split the focus between the high altar and the choir.

A new altar, made from American white oak, was introduced in 1998. For Sunday services it is positioned on the west side of the choirstalls to make worship a more intimate experience. At other times it can be seen in the Thomas à Becket Chapel.

LEFT: The west window, with its nine lights, is unusually large. It depicts in the outer lights the Apostles, in the centre the baptism of Christ. ③

HOLY TRINITY
STRATFORD-UPON-AVON

A WELCOME FROM THE VICAR

Welcome to the Collegiate Church of the Holy and Undivided Trinity, one of England's most beautiful parish churches. The people of Stratford-upon-Avon have worshipped in this building for more than 750 years. Here, every day of the year, Christians offer him praise, through his Son, Jesus Christ, and in the power of the Holy Spirit.

Holy Trinity is the church where William Shakespeare was baptized, where he worshipped and where he is buried. Thousands of visitors come each year to view his final resting place.

While you are here, please take time to wonder at the faith which led our ancestors to build this place with such skill and beauty. Feel the atmosphere of prayer and praise, an echo of the millions of prayers offered here over the centuries. Sit awhile in a place designed to make us especially aware of the love and the peace of God, and of his concern for the world.

We pray for our visitors each day. We ask you to pray for the clergy and people of Holy Trinity. May the peace of God be with you always.

ABOVE: *The avenue of lime trees leading to the north door. The trees on the left represent the tribes of Israel and those on the right the Apostles, with the holly bush for Judas and the set-back lime for Matthias.*

FRONT COVER: *The church from across the River Avon.*

A HISTORY OF CHANGE

oly Trinity Church in its garden setting by the Avon remains very much the same as it was in William Shakespeare's day.

Yet the lovely church where the great playwright lies buried has a fascinating 750-year history of change and counter-change. Most additions have served to add to its beauty and dignity; other alterations, some of which have now been swept away, have had the opposite effect.

The first mention of a local house of worship is in the charter of 845 signed by Beorthwulf, King of Mercia, granting privileges to a small minster church at Stratford. The church is likely to have been constructed of wood and was sited near to where Holy Trinity now stands, at a ford over the Avon. It was dependent on Worcester Cathedral. It is likely that the church was rebuilt in stone by the Normans but nothing remains of either construction.

The earliest records of the present church date from 1332, but it is known that the transepts were built around 1210. This original foundation was extended some years later by the Guild of the Holy Cross, founded in 1269. Primarily religious and charitable in aim, the Guild owned many local properties and used much of its income to enhance the fabric of the town. One of its masters was Robert de Stratforde, rector of Holy Trinity and later Lord Chancellor of England. Between 1280 and 1330 the Guild gave Holy Trinity the money to build aisles, nave and a tower.

In 1331, Robert's brother John, who became Archbishop of Canterbury, founded a chantry for five priests in St Thomas's Chapel in the south aisle. A chantry was an altar or chapel endowed to ensure continuing masses for donors and their families. Within 200 metres of the west door, a 'good stone house' was built for the 'College of Stratford', a regulated community of chantry priests, confirmed in its privileges by Henry V in 1415. Thereafter the church was styled 'the collegiate church' and the rector became warden of the college. Between 1480 and 1520 the chancel, clerestory, north porch, west window and tower were completed under the auspices of deans Thomas Balsall and Ralph Collingwood.

ABOVE: One of three funeral hatchments displaying the armorial bearings of a person of rank and substance. ④

LEFT: A detail from the 'American' window (1896), a gift from the people of the USA to Shakespeare's church. ⑨

RIGHT: The broken 15th-century font in which the infant William Shakespeare was probably baptized. ⑪

The nave, built of limestone from the Cotswold Hills, represents 200 years of architectural development. The pillars date from 1280, the earliest contribution of the Guild of the Holy Cross. The arches were built 100 years later and the clerestory 100 years after that. The whole represents a fine example of Perpendicular architecture.

The stained glass is mainly Victorian, as most of the medieval glass was destroyed at the Reformation. Statues in the niches above the west door disappeared at the same time. Some fragments from the glass of the chancel have been placed in the upper part of the window in the Clopton Chapel.

Many of the roof's timbers are medieval and the purlin that runs longitudinally down the middle is also original. The tie-beams which separate the 12 bays are modern.

The font is a copy of the 15th-century one in which Shakespeare was baptized. What is thought to be the original is now in the chancel.

LEFT: *A panel depicting St Helena, from the pulpit which was given in the early 1900s by Sir Theodore Martin in memory of his wife, Helen Faucit, a well-known Shakespearian actor. It is said that the carving of the saint bears a remarkable likeness to Miss Faucit!* ⑤

OPPOSITE PAGE: *The nave looking east to the organ and the chancel beyond.* ③

ABOVE: *The tomb of George Carew, Earl of Totnes and Baron Clopton (1555–1629), and Joyce, his wife, has been described as the finest Renaissance tomb in Europe. A former naval commander, he became Master in Ordnance to King James I.* ⑥

The organ has been moved several times in its history. It was originally built over the arch of the tower by Thomas Swarebrick in 1731 at a cost of £300. In 1840 it was moved to the west end. In 1889, it was enlarged by William Hill & Sons and placed in the position where we see it today. The fine woodwork that surrounds it was added at this time. The instrument's most recent rebuilding was carried out by Nicholson's in 1990–91.

The Clopton Chapel (or Lady Chapel) was dedicated to the patron saints of the local guilds, St Mary and St John. After the Reformation it became associated with the Clopton family. The altar tomb under the southern arch was prepared for Sir Hugh Clopton, benefactor to Stratford and sometime Lord Mayor of London, but he was buried in London in 1496.

Monuments to his descendants grace the other walls, notably that of William and Agnes Clopton (1592) on the north wall and, in the centre, the tomb of their son-in-law George Carew and his wife Joyce.

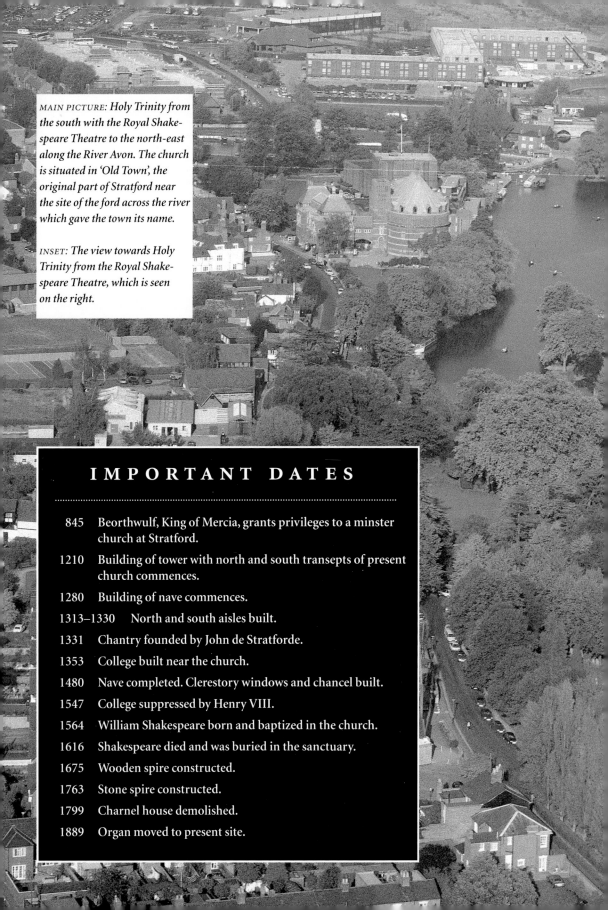

MAIN PICTURE: *Holy Trinity from the south with the Royal Shakespeare Theatre to the north-east along the River Avon. The church is situated in 'Old Town', the original part of Stratford near the site of the ford across the river which gave the town its name.*

INSET: *The view towards Holy Trinity from the Royal Shakespeare Theatre, which is seen on the right.*

IMPORTANT DATES

THE CHANCEL

The fine chancel of Holy Trinity was built in 1480 from local Warwick stone. It is dominated by the east window, which is built in the Perpendicular style. The Victorian stained glass depicts the 'Adoration of the Crucified'.

In common with several other medieval churches, Holy Trinity has a 'weeping chancel' with a displacement to the north of over 1 metre. The term refers to the position of Christ's head on the Cross. It may be that the builders of Holy Trinity intended this symbolic allusion. Perhaps the terrain was difficult or the workmen incompetent. It has been less plausibly suggested that its purpose was to make it less easy for the Devil to find the altar!

The stalls and misericords have been in continuous use for over 500 years. In the days of the College, fathers and brothers would sing the offices here, entering by the priests' door in the south wall. The misericords get their name from the carved ledge beneath each seat that allowed elderly or infirm brothers to sit while appearing to stand during the very long services (*Misericordia* is Latin for 'mercy').

Medieval carvers had considerable freedom in what they did and often seized the opportunity with relish and imagination. Their work reflects life in the 15th century and includes birds, beasts and demons, as well as most aspects of human behaviour. One misericord depicts a merman and mermaid, another a winged monster with the head of a nun and the hind quarters of a lion. A carved seat on the right near the priest's door shows a woman simultaneously pulling a man's beard, hitting him with a pan, and kicking him painfully! (see picture on opposite page).

The chancel screen is not the one through which William Shakespeare's body was carried for burial in 1616. That now stands in the crossing at the entrance to the choir vestry.

RIGHT: The chancel was built in 1480 by Dean Balsall, whose defaced tomb is situated north of the altar. The east or Te Deum *window shows the Lord adored by angels and saints, depicting the 'Adoration of the Crucified'. The roof is embellished by shields of great Warwickshire families. Shakespeare's grave is in the floor beyond the altar rail on the left, with his monument above on the wall.* ⑧

LEFT: The carved ledge of a misericord. The carvings in the choirstalls represent all manner of figures from 15th-century life: dancers, clowns, quarrellers, monkeys, fishes and strange animals.

Three items in the chancel carry with them a particularly interesting and chequered history. Near Shakespeare's tomb is a broken font that dates from the 15th century. This is almost certainly the one in which the infant William was baptized. It was probably removed in the 17th century when the Puritan zeal of Cromwell's Commonwealth was at its height, but saved from total destruction by Thomas Paine, the Parish Clerk, who died in 1747. Having for some years been used as a cattle trough, it was found in a local garden and restored to the chancel in 1823, albeit in broken form.

The Purbeck marble altar stone spent centuries under the floor in the church. It is the slab from the original altar in the Chapel of St Thomas and still bears four of the five consecration crosses traditionally inscribed on altar stones to represent the five wounds of Christ. During the Reformation it was removed and in the late 19th century restored to a refurbished high altar.

The chained Bible on display in the chancel is an example of the first edition of the King James Authorized Version, printed in London in 1611 in the old Gothic type. It was stolen in 1984, but quickly recovered by the police, perhaps the first time it had left the building in more than 350 years.

ABOVE: A poignant memorial on the north side of the chancel commemorates two 17th-century lovers. Judith Coombe died in 1649 shortly before her marriage to Richard, who erected the memorial to immortalize their love.

SHAKESPEARE'S CHURCH

William Shakespeare, considered by many to be the greatest playwright of all time, had a lifelong connection with Stratford and with Holy Trinity Church. He was baptized here on 26 April 1564 and educated in the town. He left for London in 1585 but paid frequent visits home, returning to settle in 1611, having built up considerable estates here. He died on 23 April 1616, the 52nd anniversary of his birth, and is buried in the chancel. His wife, daughter and son-in-law lie beside him.

ABOVE: The memorial above William Shakespeare's grave. ⑫

LEFT: Flowers laid around the grave during the playwright's birthday celebrations weekend, an annual event. ⑫

Shakespeare's entitlement to be buried in Holy Trinity is nothing to do with his celebrity as a playwright. Rather it stems from the fact that he was a 'lay rector' of this church. The title did not imply any priestly function but rather was one given to long-term benefactors. In 1605, Shakespeare bought for £440 a lease on a moiety (half-share) of the tithes (taxes) due to certain local churches. With the lay rectorship came the privilege of burial in the church. In return the playwright was obliged to help keep the chancel in good repair during his lifetime. The poor condition of the fabric recorded not long after his death suggests that he was not too assiduous in carrying out this duty.

ABOVE: An extract from the Parish Register recording the burial of William Shakespeare on 25 April 1616. It reads 'Will Shakespear, gent'. ⑪

LEFT: The resting-place of William Shakespeare. ⑫

The memorial on the wall above Shakespeare's grave was sculpted by Gerard Johnson (or Janssen) within a few years of the playwright's death. It was restored in 1974 after careful research into its original colouration. Apparently Shakespeare's somewhat sunburnt appearance is in keeping with the original colouration. The memorial was completed in his widow's lifetime, and we may therefore assume it to be a close likeness.

The tomb in the corner beyond, also sculpted by Johnson, is of John Combe, a friend of Shakespeare who left him a legacy of £6 a year. On the north wall of the chancel, close to where William Shakespeare and his family are buried, is a walled-up doorway which was not blocked in the playwright's time. This led to a charnel house, a three-storey building in which were piled bones that had been removed from the chancel and the graveyard in order to make room for others to be buried. It is quite possible that the playwright may have witnessed such an exhumation and decided that it was not for him. Hence the epitaph on his gravestone, reproduced below.

God shall be truly known …
Our children's children shall see this,
and bless heaven.

WILLIAM SHAKESPEARE, HENRY VIII ACT V SC. 5

GOOD FREND FOR IESVS SAKE FORBEARE,
TO DIGG HE DVST ENCLOASED HEARE.
BLESE BE Ye MAN Yt SPARES HES STONES,
AND CVRST BE HE Yt MOVES MY BONES.

LEFT: The 'curse' on Shakespeare's grave. Such epitaphs were not uncommon. ⑫

THE CHURCH TODAY

Well over three hundred people worship in Holy Trinity each Sunday. The church fills to capacity at many special services and at the great Christian festivals of Christmas and Easter. Daily, Morning and Evening Prayer are said throughout the year. However many or few join in worship, we keep faith with the purpose of those who built Holy Trinity. They toiled to offer a place for the faithful of Stratford to worship Almighty God. Their worship was a part of the rhythm of life and included times of joy and sorrow, of excitement and fear. The offering of praise to God remains the reason for this church's existence today. From here, each Sunday, Christians go out to witness to the love of God in their daily lives.

It is inevitable, however, that William Shakespeare continues to play a role in Holy Trinity's life, nearly 400 years after his death. His final resting place is inside the church, which is why Stratford's parish church is probably the most visited parish church in the country. We have more visitors than many of our great cathedrals. This adds a dimension to our worshipping life which is both challenging and welcome.

Many of our visitors come solely to view Shakespeare's grave, not realizing that this is a living place of worship. Many assume it to be an ecclesiastical museum. Our hope and prayer is that they, and all our visitors, will pause to find something beyond the building. It is a joy and a privilege to have such a fine building as our spiritual home where we 'worship the Lord in the beauty of his holiness' (Psalms 29.2 and 96.9).

We want you to experience the 'holy' in this holy place. You may be surprised to find yourself feeling a sense of awe, of mystery, of something holy beyond. It is here that some have discovered their own longing for God. That is the process of spiritual growth from visitor to pilgrim. If you have already thought of yourself as

being on a Christian pilgrimage, then linger to pray, that pilgrimage might become discipleship, in the love and service of our Lord Jesus Christ. May the God of peace fill you with all joy and hope in believing, and may his blessing rest upon you, always.

ABOVE: *A Sunday service in progress.*